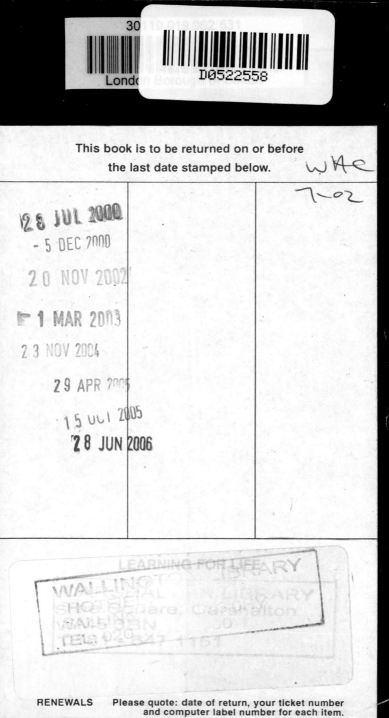

For my son
Nicholas James Tulloch,
who is *never* alone.

Oxford University Press, Great Clarendon Street.
Oxford OX2 6DP

Oxford   New York
Athens   Auckland   Bangkok   Bogotá   Buenos Aires
Calcutta   Cape Town   Chennai   Dar es Salaam
Delhi   Florence   Hong Kong   Istanbul   Karachi
Kuala Lumpur Madrid   Melbourne   Mexico City
Mumbai   Nairobi   Paris   São Paulo   Singapore
Taipei   Tokyo   Toronto   Warsaw

and associated companies in
Berlin   Ibadan

Oxford is a trade mark of Oxford University Press

Text copyright © Nicholas Tulloch 1997
Illustrations copyright © Chris Mould 1997
First published 1997
Reprinted in paperback 1998

Nicholas Tulloch and Chris Mould have asserted their
moral right to be identified as the authors of this work.

A CIP catalogue record for this book is available
from the British Library

ISBN 0 19 276155 2 (hardback)
ISBN 0 19 276156 0 (paperback)

Printed in Hong Kong

HA HA HA

ALPHABET SPOOK!

SPINE-TINGLING VERSE

written by

Nicholas Tulloch

Illustrated by

Chris Mould

OXFORD UNIVERSITY PRESS

OXFORD NEW YORK TORONTO

Contents

Alphabet Spook!

A is for Aaargh! And **B** is for Bat,
C is for Cauldron and witch's black Cat.
D is for Demon who hides in the park,
E is for Entity waiting till dark.
F is for Frankenstein seven feet tall,
G is for Ghostie who walks through my wall.
H is for Horrible thing in my room,
I is for 'I'm getting out of here soon!'
J is for Jump, and that's what I do most,
K is for Kissing the ghost for some toast.
L is for Lab where the creatures are made,
M is for Monster who lives in the shade.
N is for Noises I hear all around,

O is for Ogre who stays underground.
P is for Phantom, and if he should come,
Q is for 'Quick!'
And **R** is for 'Run!'
S is for Spirit who always is near,
T is for Terrible moans that you'll hear.
U is for Under the floorboards you'll see,
V is for Vampire, that's where he'll be.
W is for Werewolf who's full of strange cries,
X is for 'X-Ray', the man with weird eyes.
Y is for Yeti I'd see in the snow,
And **Z** is for Zombie, if he'd LET ME GO!

Ankle-biter

Ankle-biter waits
Below the stair.
And all who pass
Had best look out,
Had best beware.
For Ankle-biter *always*
Likes to shock.
So if you find yourself
Upon the stair;
Beware! (And wear thick socks.)

Apparition Superstition

Apparition Superstition's
A tradition where I'm livin'
So I'm givin' all my mirrors
To the man I've saved them for.
His name is Mister Drac, you know
He cannot see himself, and so
I'm hoping he's so puzzled,
He'll forget *I* live next door!

Banshee Blues

I've got the Banshee Blues.
She follows me
All over town
And all around,
It's got me feeling down.

I've got the Banshee Blues.
She won't be quiet
In my mind
I always find,
She's not the quiet kind.

I've got the Banshee Blues.
I've got to get her
Off my tail.
She's off the rails,
Begone, Princess of Wails!

Bogy Man

Said the Bogy Man
To the rest of his clan,
'An unfortunate name
We have chose.
When they're calling me *Bogy*,
They think I'm a fogy
Who just likes to play
With his nose.'

Confront Your Demons

'Confront your demons,'
Said Doctor Yansoff,
Meaning, (and I plainly speak)
That Monsters, though they make you shriek,
Ought not to make you scare your pantsoff.

Cyclops

One eye on me,
One eye on you,
He'll always be the same,
He's got one eye on *everyone*,
For Cyclops is his name.

Drip! Drop!

Drip! Drop!
Drip! Drop!
Something's leaking, I'll go fetch a mop.
But what could it be? I can't quite be sure,
I've never heard dripping *that* drippy before.
It might be a demon who hides in the dark,
Who'll gobble me up for a bit of a lark.
Or if I'm unlucky, he'll eat me for fun,
With a large box of fries and a sesame bun.
I really don't want to get out of my bed,
'Cos laughing-boy's waiting to bite off my head!
I'll bet his idea of a bit of a joke,
Is washing me down with a big glass of Coke!
And when he's all finished, he'll curl up and sleep,
Leaving my bones on the floor in a heap.
Though my story is over, keep listening my friend,
For if you hear dripping, it could be; THE END.

(Unless it's just a leaky tap, of course.)

Drac is Back!

The Mummy's gone, the Ghost's been fired,
The Werewolf's packed up and retired,
The Gremlins now, won't be re-hired,
For Drac
Is back
In town.

The Gorgon's going underground,
The Swamp Beast's in the Lost and Found,
Poor Frankenstein has lost his crown,
For Drac
Is back
In town.

Six hundred years he's been away,
But now he's back, there's hell to pay,
It's *his* turn now to have his say,
For Drac
Is back
In town.

Forget the Alien, he's a fake,
The Prince of Darkness is awake,
So grab your crucifix and stake,
For Drac
Is back
In town.

Ectoplasm

The Ectoplasm is a glue,
A kind of tacky, ghostly goo,
On no account become his friend,
Unless you'd like a sticky end.

Egor

I knew a man called Egor,
Who lived up on the hill,
'It's getting cold,' he said to me,
'Come in, you'll catch a chill.'

I had my reservations,
But he implored me still,
'Surprises I can promise,
If we both go up the hill.'

And when we were up
We were up.
And when we were down
I heard a yell,
And when we were only
Half-way up,
I turned and ran like hell!

Frankenstein, Frankenstein

Frankenstein, Frankenstein,
Where have you been?
'I've been down to London
To visit the queen.'
Frankenstein, Frankenstein,
What did you there?
'Nothing. You don't seriously think they let
Me in, do you? Look at me. I'm seven feet tall
With corners on my head…'

Fright Night

Are *you* going out
On Fright Night?
I am.
Who cares what
Lurks in the dark?
I don't.
Who'll be scared
Of a werewolf's bark?
I won't.
Who'll scream when
The Mummy moans?
I shan't.
Who can imagine
Running home?
I can't.
Are *you* going out
On Fright Night?
I am. (Not!)

Ghostly Goldfish

Ghostly Goldfish
Brave and bold fish,
How I love
Your grace and guile.
Not for you
Atlantic Ocean,
That, I'm sure,
Would cramp your style.

Ghostly Goldfish
Wet and cold fish
You're the one
I love the most.
And I'm sorry,
That I had you,
On that piece
Of buttered toast.

Ghoulfriend

I've got myself a Ghoulfriend,
I think that she's okay,
But when I ask my friends around,
She frightens them away.

They say she walks through objects
Her eyes are bleak and black,
They phone me up and tell me,
They're never coming back.

They say they hate the screaming,
And all the ghostly wails,
But still I don't believe them,
I'm sure they're telling tales.

And still they say I'm foolish,
True love they say, I lack,
But when my Ghoul gives me the eye,
I *always* give it back.

Hallowe'en

Come out,
Come out,
On Hallowe'en!
The weirdest things
You've ever seen,
Are right before
Your very eyes,
Surprise, surprise,
On Hallowe'en!

Come out,
Come out,
And see them play!
The Goblins dance
The night away,
And things once dead,
Will now arise,
Surprise, surprise,
On Hallowe'en!

Come out,
Come out,
And be the first!
The witch's brew
Will quench your thirst,
Come now before
October dies,
Surprise, surprise,
On Hallowe'en!

Harry's Hob-nailed Boots

'These boots are just atrocious!'
Said Harry Jones one day,
His language was ferocious,
His boots were in dismay.

Then Harry cursed the leather,
And said, 'I'll make you learn,
Too long we've stayed together,
So now, boots, you will burn!'

'I've heard the way you're talking,'
Said Harry's hob-nailed boots,
And so they went out walking,
With Harry in pursuit.

Outside, the rain was falling,
But still the boots walked on,
In vain was Harry calling,
For Harry's boots
Were gone.

Invisible John

Invisible John,
Invisible John,
I'm getting the blame
For the things you've
    done.
You tease the girls
And pull their hair,
They turn around,
I'm standing there.
You call them names,
And they see red,
I hate it when
They punch my head.
You steal the apples
From the stall,
The grocer isn't
Pleased at all.
He said that next time
I do that,
Then like a bug
He'll squash me flat.

Miss Williams
Has called me now,
She's looking puzzled,
Wonders how,
I managed,
From way over *there*,
To put a stink bomb
On her chair.
All right, all right!
You've made the most,
Of your position
As a ghost.
Now go away
And leave me be.
Two's company?
I don't agree!
Invisible John,
Invisible John,
I'm getting the blame
For the things you've
    done.

I Saw Eyesore

I saw Eyesore
You saw Eyesore
We saw Eyesore
Late last night.
Eyesore said,
'My stomach's hurting!'
Eyesore didn't
Feel too bright.

I said, 'Eyesore,
Please tell, why sore?
Do confide,
Monstrosity.'
'I've just scoffed someone,'
Said Eyesore,
'Who did not
Agree with me!'

Joking Joe

Have *you* seen Joking Joe?
He always used to scare us,
And trick or treat and dare us.
He'd hide behind the doors,
Jumping out,
With a shout.
He thought it was a joke,
Funny bloke.

Have *you* seen Joking Joe?
At first he would ignore us,
But in the end he'd bore us,
With all those stupid pranks.
So uncool,
Played the fool,
Till Dracula was hired.
Joe expired.

Have *you* seen Joking Joe?
We haven't.
Honest!

Just a Minute

Just a minute.
Was that the creaking of a door,
Or is it in my mind?
Funny really, innit?
All the things you think you'll find.

Just a minute.
Is there something in the gloom,
Boggy-eyed and straggly-haired?
Spooky really, innit?
How the night can make you scared.

King Conga

King Conga
Climbed up the building
With the girl
In his arms.
But still they turned up
In their planes.
Shot him down
In flames.
Poor King Conga.
Never gave him a chance.
Probably only wanted
To dance.

Knightmare
(in Shining Armour)

He used to be
My worst knightmare
In shining armour.
He would climb the long,
Long,
Winding stair
To where I slept.
My mind was kept
From simple things
Like birds and trees,
For both of these
Meant nothing.
With his ghostly rattling,
And his clanking,
He preyed
Upon my fears,
For all those years,
Until…

He lost his footing
On the stair.
How did he fall?
I do not care.
CLANK! THUD! BANG!
CRASH! RATTLE! CLANG!
At the foot of the stair
He lay.
Nothing but a tin can,
Squashed flat.
I wouldn't even put
Sardines in that.

Luminous Larry

Luminous Larry
Would flash in the night,
His mother's excuse was,
'He's always been bright!'
But Larry was bored
And he started a search,
To be rid of the glowing,
And phoned up the church.

The vicar said, 'Larry,
It could be a sign,
Of some inspirational
Matter divine!'
But sadly it wasn't,
And so the archdeacon,
Got Larry a job
As a Belisha beacon. (Amen)

Lurking in the Bog

There is a grisly creature,
He's lurking in the bog,
And when he's done
He'll pull the chain,
And drift back through the fog.

My Brother is a Werewolf

My brother didn't always,
Gnash his teeth at night,
But now he just can't help it,
It doesn't seem quite right.

My brother didn't always,
Go prowling on the moors,
He *loved* his stamp collection,
Until he grew those claws.

He's even started drooling,
And speaking with a slur,
And every Sunday morning,
His bed is full of fur.

My mum says I should love him,
And always treat him right,
I've got a dribbling sibling,
Who loves the pale moonlight.

My Fire Started Dancing the Tango

While staring at my fireplace,
One cold and lonely night,
I viewed an awesome spectacle,
Which gave me quite a fright.
I thought that I was dreaming,
But I'll swear I saw it right,
My fire started dancing the tango.

I sat up to attention,
And I found to my surprise,
That several yellow flames
Were waltzing right before my eyes,
The blue-ish flames were minueting
Fast as they could rise,
My fire started dancing the tango.

The red flames bossa nova'd
While the poker played a beat,
The ashes, after rising,
Stood in line and tapped their feet.
The shovel on piano,
Made the line-up quite complete.
My fire started dancing the tango.

No-head's Revenge

Though they chopped off his block
On that wintry morn,
He declared, 'There's no need for alarm!'
'I will not lose my head,'
Were the last words he said,
So he carries it under his arm.

Nicholas James

Nicholas James
Is alone
In the dark,
He hears a
Cat's yowl,
He hears a
Dog's bark.
But still he
Fears nothing,
Alone in the dark.

Nicholas James
Is never alone,
For Super-heroes
By the score,
Will guard the
Gifted youngster's
Door.
X-Men keep him
From all danger,
(Better than a
Power Ranger)
And Gambit holds
The winning hand
In Nicholas James's
Slumber Land.

Ogre

An Ogre took up yoga
Just to keep his body trim,
And dressed in Roman clothes
To look attractive,
On a whim.
But everybody laughed out loud
And said, 'Just look at him!'
And now that silly
Yoga Ogre's toga's in the bin.

Only You

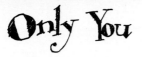

Do you awake
On humid nights
After wrestling
A Devil?
You look all around
The bedroom,
And there's
Only you.
Am I right?

Do you think
That if you
Go back to sleep,
The Thing will
Invade your thoughts,
But then when you awake
He'll be gone, leaving
Only you?
Am I right?

If so, then who's that *crouching over there*?

Poltergeist Patrol

The Poltergeist Patrol,
Is watching us tonight,
And side by side they stroll, my dear,
Under the palest light.

They never walk alone,
They're always two by two,
I'd love to walk you home unless,
They're coming after *you*.

Polly's Gone?

I once had a parrot,
Of green,
And blue,
And yellow,
And red.
But then one night
Of deathly doom,
Someone crept into
My parrot's room.
He frightened poor Polly
Right out of her wits,
And so the next morning,
We found her in bits.
But I picked up the bits,
And stuck them together,
Now Polly and I,
Are together forever.

I once had a parrot,
Of green,
And blue,
And yellow,
And red.
I now have a parrot,
Who's green,
And blue,
And yellow,
And *dead*.

Quentin Drew

Quentin Drew,
Oh, Quentin Drew,
What on earth
Are we to do?
For not much longer
Can we take,
The way that you've been
Changing shape.
From mouse to trap
And sheep to dog,
From cow to slip
And bull to frog.
From pig to sty
And door to mat,
From bed to bug
And rug to rat.

From wheel to barrow,
Toad to stool,
From coat to hook
And slide to rule.
From jam to jar
And sea to shell,
From shoe to shop
And bar to bell.
But nature has a curious wit,
So show no disrespect to it;
For it's too late, to re-arrange
Your features,
Once the wind has changed.

Quirk

The Quirk lives in a marsh,
And (let us not be harsh),
He's usually without blame,
Until you call him names.
'Quirky'
'Lurky'
'Jerky'
'Berk'
That's how you like to tease,
And Quirk is such a
Sensitive beast,
So do not tease him,
PLEASE!

Really?

'There is a beast
Behind that door.'
'Really?'
'Is it your life
You're frightened for?'
'Clearly!'
'And how much do
You value it?'
'Dearly!'
'And are your nerves
Now shot to bits?'
'Nearly!'
'How often are you
APRIL FOOLED?'

'Er, yearly...'

Run!

He's on the landing,
Run!
You dare not look
Behind the wardrobe,
There he's standing,
Run!

He's just a demon,
Run!
He's dark and deadly,
Don't just stand there,
Stop your screaming,
Run!

He's near the window,
Run!
Don't be ashamed
Of being scared,
It's not a sin so,
Run!

He's round the bend so
Run!
You see him now,
You know that it,
Could be the end so,
Run!

He's started crawling,
Run!
Your heart is pounding,
Sweat is pouring,
It's appalling,
Run!

His jaw's dropped wider,
Run!
You're terrified,
So don't deny it,
You hate that *spider*,
Run!

Smelly Ghosties

I'll have you know,
I've heard it said,
That spooks are fond,
Of garlic bread,
And what annoys me,
Now the most is,
Smelly ghosties'
Halitosis.

Snowman (ie Abominable)

Abominable Snowman,
Will stay out
In the snow, man.
His attitude is
'So, man?
Who cares if I catch cold?'
Unlike his cousin Yeti,
Who can't stand
Getting wetti,
And it's a certain
Betti,
He'd never be so bold.

Things that Go 'Bump!'

It's strange, but the moment
I turn out the light,
I get frightened by things
That go 'Bump!' in the night,
And the darkness itself
Seems to laugh with delight
At the things that go 'Bump!' in the night.

A rattling window,
A bang on the door,
A knock on the wall
And a thump on the floor,
It must be those beasties
I keep in my drawer!
They're the things that go 'Bump!' in the night.

Troll

Let us examine
The humble Troll,
And every one of his virtues
Extol…

…All right then,
I can't think of any!
I should have known
There wouldn't be many.
His body is short
And he growls a lot,
His belly is round
And resembles a pot.
He's covered in hair,
And pretty, he's not.
But listen…
I'll tell you what.

If you laid him across
The foot of the door,
(Yes, I *know* that's not
What a Troll is for.)
This odd little man,
Who could not be ruder,
Would make the perfect
Draught excluder.

Ug

Ug,
Ug,
Lives
Under
The
Plug,
Not in the bedroom,
Or
Under the rug.
And if he grips you
In his icy hug,
Your final words
Will be

Glug Glug Glug

Under My Bed

Under my bed
Is a monstrous creature,
My sister described
His every feature.
His teeth are black, his eyes are red,
He fills me with the darkest dread.
His ears are gnarled, his tongue is green,
He really is a nasty fiend.
I hope he never captures me,
For that would be a tragedy.
He'd grunt and growl, and crush my bones,
Ignoring all my fearful groans.

But then again,
To tell the truth,
I've never actually
Seen the brute.
I take my sister's word for it,
About this creature and his pit.
Now is she telling
Little lies,
And making
Sneaky alibis?
She's eager that I get out soon;
Does she want my safety,
Or
My
Room?

Vampire Cat

The Vampire Cat,
Is there anyone that,
Is as feared by the people
As he?
Does it ever occur
That if they stroked his fur,
He'd be pleasant
As pleasant can be?

But it's always a shame,
It's a different game,
When his vampiring muscles
He'll flex.
He'll still drink their milk,
And all drinks of that ilk,
But for afters,
He's after their necks!

Vulture

Vulture
Circling overhead.
Watching,
Waiting,
Watching,
Waiting.
Vulture
Always biding time.
Watching,
Waiting,
Watching,
Waiting.

It's your destiny
To wait,
And forever
Hesitate.
Though I marvel
At your beauty,
You possess
A sense of duty.
And to prove
My love is real,
I'll *gladly* be
Your latest meal.

Which was the Witch?

Which was the witch
Who prepared that stew?
Which was the witch
That boiled it?
She didn't put
The frogspawn in,
And now she's gone
And spoiled it!

'Wrong', Said Fred

Late one night
In the dead of the dark,
Fred and I
Sneaked into the park.
We'd both agreed,
And made a pact,
That all things evil
Should be tracked.
We'd nail the goblins
To a tree,
'Monstrosities are
   history!'
These words became our
   battle cry,
'Let's do,' said Fred,
'Or die!'

Then, said Fred,
(These words I feared),
'I'm feeling odd,
I'm feeling weird.'
And in the darkness
I could see
That something stood
In front of me.

And in the gloom
I said to Fred,
'Let's leave before we
   end up dead,
It's time to go, the hour's
   late.'
'Hold on,' said Fred,
'Just wait.'

Then, said Fred,
'What would you say,
If you were told
Upon this day,
Each monster is
A living thing,
Which hates the misery
You bring?'
Fred's face was grey,
His hands were cold,
His eyes were black, and
   I was told,
'A nightmare is the worst
   you'll see?
Wrong,' said Fred,
'It's *ME*!'

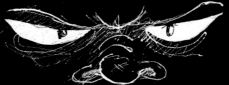

'X' Marks the Spot

'X' marks the spot
Where the whole thing took place,
But we've looked all around
And he's gone without trace.
Someone reported
The cries of a beast,
But the evidence shows
There's no beast in the least.

This is a mystery
Still incomplete,
All that we've found's
What he wore on his feet.
And we'll never know
What can make a man choose,
To jump out of his wits,
And then out of his shoes.

X-Ray

X-Ray
Is looking through you.
He sees your
Inner soul,
And though you try
To shut him out,
He'll always reach
His goal.
You'll always lose
To X-Ray,
He'll always be
The winner.
I do suppose,
He even knows,
What you've just had
For dinner!

Yet Again

Yet again
I'm last in bed,
This worries me,
It hurts my head.
It means *I* must
Turn out the light
And then towards my bed
Take flight.
And though the journey's
Only short,
I must be careful,
I'm not caught.

Here goes. Goodnight... Yow!!

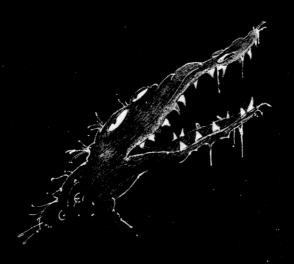

(Not) Yetis

So much fun are Yetis,
They really are a scre-am,
They use the snow as camouflage,
Just so that you can't see 'em.

Zebediah Morgan

Zebediah Morgan
Lived with a bat,
Boiled his soup
In an old top hat,
Spent his time
With no one at all,
Kept ten pence
In a hole in the wall.
Stayed in bed
Till late afternoon,
Cleaned his ears
With a rusty spoon.
Combed his hair
With an old fish bone,
Picked his teeth
With a sharpened stone.
Washed his feet
In Irish stew,
Stuck back falling
Hair with glue.
Died last week
Mysteriously,
Left not a penny
To the bat,
Or me.

Zeds

The Zeds inside your head,
Make you want to
Go to bed.
You know you'll dream
Of all the things,
That every wicked
Nightmare brings.
But Zeds are really
All you need,
So never try to fight them.
Just go ahead,
Invite them.